Best - ever
BROWNIES

It's never the wrong time for brownies

THE AUSTRALIAN
Women's Weekly

contents

You know you're about to eat something special when it has a national day named after it. Each year on December 8th the US celebrates 'National Brownie Day'. We love them here, too. They're easy to make and, whether they're fudgy or cake-like, we think they all deserve a brownie point because of the big, rich, chocolatey hit they give.

Pamela Clark

Editorial & Food Director

chocolate

Brownies are so-named because of their rich, dark brown colour; brownies without chocolate (or those that use white chocolate) are known as blondies.

triple chocolate brownies

- **125g (4 ounces) butter, chopped**
- **200g (6½ ounces) dark (semi-sweet) chocolate, chopped coarsely**
- **½ cup (110g) caster (superfine) sugar**
- **2 eggs, beaten lightly**
- **1¼ cups (185g) plain (all-purpose) flour**
- **150g (4½ ounces) white chocolate, chopped coarsely**
- **100g (3 ounces) milk chocolate, chopped coarsely**

1 Preheat oven to 180°C/350°F. Grease a deep 19cm (8-inch) square cake pan; line base and sides with baking paper, extending paper 5cm (2 inches) above sides of pan.

2 Combine butter and dark chocolate in a medium saucepan; stir over low heat until melted. Cool 10 minutes.

3 Stir in sugar and egg, then sifted flour until combined; stir in white and milk chocolates. Spread mixture into pan.

4 Bake for 35 minutes or until mixture is firm to touch. Cool brownie in pan. Sprinkle with sifted cocoa powder or icing sugar before cutting, if you like.

serves 12
prep + cook time
1 hour (+ cooling)

Tip Brownies can be made 4 days ahead; store in an airtight container.

makes 32
prep + cook time
50 minutes (+ cooling)

Tip For an easy sour cream frosting, melt 100g (3 ounces) dark chocolate, cool slightly, then fold it into ¼ cup sour cream.

mini chocolate brownies

- 125g (4 ounces) butter, chopped
- 200g (6½ ounces) dark (semi-sweet) chocolate, chopped coarsely
- ¾ cup (165g) caster (superfine) sugar
- 1 teaspoon vanilla extract
- 2 eggs, beaten lightly
- 1 cup (150g) plain (all-purpose) flour

1 Preheat oven to 180°C/350°F. Grease a deep 19cm (8-inch) square cake pan; line base and two sides with baking paper, extending paper 5cm (2 inches) above sides of pan.

2 Stir butter and chocolate in a medium heatproof bowl over a medium saucepan of simmering water until smooth (don't let water touch base of bowl). Remove from heat; stir in sugar and extract, then egg and sifted flour. Pour mixture into pan.

3 Bake for 30 minutes or until just firm. Cool brownie in pan.

4 Turn brownie onto a board; cut into 16 squares then cut into triangles.

tip Store brownies in an airtight container for up to 4 days. To freeze, wrap in plastic then foil; freeze for up to 3 months.

choc brownie muffins

- 2 cups (300g) self-raising flour
- ⅓ cup (35g) cocoa powder
- ⅓ cup (75g) caster (superfine) sugar
- 60g (2 ounces) butter, melted
- ½ cup (95g) dark choc Bits
- ½ cup (75g) pistachios, chopped coarsely
- ½ cup (165g) chocolate hazelnut spread (Nutella)
- 1 egg, beaten lightly
- ¾ cup (180ml) milk
- ½ cup (120g) sour cream

1 Preheat oven to 200°C/400°F. Grease a 12-hole (⅓-cup/80ml) muffin pan.
2 Sift dry ingredients into a large bowl; stir in the remaining ingredients (be careful not to over-mix). Divide mixture evenly into pan holes.
3 Bake about 20 minutes. Stand muffins in pan for 5 minutes before turning, top-side up, onto a wire rack to cool. Dust with sifted extra cocoa before serving, if you like.

tips Take care not to overcook the muffins – they should be slightly moist in the middle. They can be made a day ahead and stored in an airtight container, or freeze for up to 3 months.

makes 12
prep + cook time 35 minutes

Tip *Brownies will keep in an airtight container at room temperature for 4 days; in the refrigerator for 1 week; or frozen for up to 2 months.*

choc-mint brownies

- 200g (6½ ounces) dark (semi-sweet) chocolate
- 125g (4 ounces) butter, chopped coarsely
- 200g (6½ ounces) dark (semi-sweet) chocolate, extra, chopped coarsely
- ½ cup (110g) caster (superfine) sugar
- 2 eggs, beaten lightly
- 1¼ cups (185g) plain (all-purpose) flour
- 6 mint patties (120g), chopped coarsely

1 Preheat oven to 180°C/350°F. Grease a deep 19cm (8-inch) square cake pan; line base and sides with baking paper, extending paper 5cm (2 inches) above sides of pan.
2 Melt chocolate in a medium heatproof bowl over a medium saucepan of simmering water (don't let water touch base of bowl). Spread melted chocolate evenly over base of pan; cover, refrigerate until set.
3 Meanwhile, stir butter and chopped chocolate in a medium saucepan over low heat until smooth. Remove from heat; stir in sugar. Cool 10 minutes.
4 Stir in egg, then sifted flour. Stir in mint patties. Spread mixture into pan.
5 Bake brownie about 30 minutes. Cool in pan; refrigerate for 30 minutes to set the chocolate on the brownie base again.
6 Turn brownie, top-side up, onto board. Cut into nine squares; cut squares into triangles.

chocolate fudge brownies

- 150g (4½ ounces) butter
- 300g (9½ ounces) dark (semi-sweet) chocolate, chopped coarsely
- 1½ cups (330g) firmly packed brown sugar
- 3 eggs
- 2 teaspoons vanilla extract
- ¾ cup (110g) plain (all-purpose) flour
- ¾ cup (140g) dark choc Bits
- ½ cup (120g) sour cream
- ¾ cup (110g) macadamias, toasted, chopped coarsely
- cocoa powder, for dusting

1 Preheat oven to 180°C/350°F. Grease 19cm x 29cm (8-inch x 12-inch) rectangular slice pan; line base and two long sides with baking paper, extending paper 2cm (¾ inch) above sides of pan.

2 Melt butter in a medium saucepan, add chocolate; stir over low heat until mixture is smooth. Stir in sugar, then transfer mixture to a large bowl; cool until just warm.

3 Stir in eggs, one at a time, then stir in extract, sifted flour, choc Bits, sour cream and nuts. Spread mixture into pan.

4 Bake for 40 minutes. Cover pan with foil, bake for a further 20 minutes.

5 Cool brownie in pan. Turn top-side up onto a wire rack; dust with sifted cocoa. Cut into 12 pieces to serve.

makes 12
prep + cook time
1½ hours (+ cooling)

Tips Store brownies in the refrigerator for up to 1 week. This recipe produces a brownie that's a happy medium between fudgy and cake-like. Reduce the baking time by 10 minutes for a more moist brownie.

tips Make this into a white chocolate blondie by replacing the brown sugar with caster (superfine) sugar. Blondie can be made 3 days ahead; store in an airtight container.

egg-free butterscotch blondies

This recipe is egg- and nut-free.

- 150g (4½ ounces) butter, chopped coarsely
- 180g (5½ ounces) white chocolate, chopped coarsely
- ¾ cup (180ml) milk
- ¾ cup (165g) firmly packed brown sugar
- 1 teaspoon dried yeast
- 1½ cups (225g) plain (all-purpose) flour
- ⅓ cup (55g) pure icing (confectioners') sugar
- ⅓ cup (65g) dark choc Bits
- ⅓ cup (65g) caramel choc Bits
- ⅓ cup (65g) white choc Bits

1 Preheat oven to 160°C/325°F. Grease a 20cm x 30cm (8-inch x 12-inch) rectangular slice pan; line base and sides with baking paper, extending paper 2cm (¾ inch) above sides of pan.

2 Stir butter, chopped chocolate and milk in a large saucepan over medium heat until mixture is smooth. Remove from heat. Add brown sugar and yeast; stir to combine. Cool for 5 minutes.

3 Whisk sifted flour and icing sugar into chocolate mixture. Fold through half the combined choc Bits.

4 Pour mixture into pan. Sprinkle with remaining choc Bits.

5 Bake for 40 minutes or until blondie is golden brown and just cooked through. Cool blondie in pan before cutting into rectangles.

makes 20
prep + cook time
1 hour (+ cooling)

gluten-free chocolate cheesecake brownie

This recipe is gluten-, dairy-, nut- and yeast-free.

- 150g (4½ ounces) dairy-free dark chocolate, chopped coarsely
- 150g (4½ ounces) dairy-free spread
- 1¼ cups (275g) caster (superfine) sugar
- 2 eggs, beaten lightly
- 2 teaspoons vanilla extract
- ½ cup (75g) tapioca flour
- ½ cup (65g) gluten-free self-raising flour
- ⅓ cup (35g) dutch cocoa powder
- 227g (7 ounces) tofutti 'better than cream cheese', softened (see tip)
- 1 tablespoon caster (superfine) sugar, extra

1 Preheat oven to 160°C/325°F. Grease a deep 22cm (9-inch) square cake pan; line base and sides with baking paper, extending paper 5cm (2 inches) above sides of pan.

2 Stir chocolate and dairy-free spread in a medium saucepan over low heat until smooth. Remove from heat; cool for 5 minutes.

3 Stir sugar into chocolate mixture; add egg and half the extract, stir to combine. Stir in sifted flours and cocoa until combined. Pour mixture into pan.

4 Combine tofutti, extra sugar and remaining extract in a small bowl. Drop large spoonfuls of tofutti mixture over chocolate mixture. Use a knife to gently swirl to create a marble pattern.

5 Bake for 1¼ hours or until a skewer inserted in the centre comes out clean. Cool brownie in pan before cutting into squares.

tip Tofutti is a dairy-free soy-based product available in the refrigerator section of supermarkets and health food stores.

makes 24
prep + cook time
1½ hours (+ cooling)

Tip Store brownie in the refrigerator for up to 1 week.

choc brownies
with sour cream frosting

- **125g (4 ounces) butter, chopped coarsely**
- **185g (6 ounces) dark (semi-sweet) chocolate, chopped coarsely**
- **1 cup (220g) caster (superfine) sugar**
- **2 teaspoons vanilla extract**
- **2 eggs, beaten lightly**
- **1 cup (150g) plain (all-purpose) flour**
- **½ cup (60g) coarsely chopped pecans**

sour cream frosting

- **100g (3 ounces) dark eating (semi-sweet) chocolate, chopped coarsely**
- **¼ cup (60g) sour cream**

1 Preheat oven to 180°C/350°F. Grease a deep 19cm (8-inch) square cake pan; line base and sides with baking paper, extending paper 5cm (2 inches) above sides of pan.

2 Place butter and chocolate in a small saucepan; stir over low heat until melted. Transfer mixture to a large bowl. Stir in sugar and extract, then egg, sifted flour and nuts. Pour mixture into pan.

3 Bake about 30 minutes or until set. Cool brownie in pan.

4 Make sour cream frosting. Turn brownie out of pan; spread top with frosting. Refrigerate until set before cutting.

sour cream frosting

Melt chocolate in a small heatproof bowl over a small saucepan of simmering water (don't let water touch base of bowl). Stir in sour cream until frosting is smooth and glossy.

makes 16
prep + cook time
55 minutes (+ cooling & refrigeration)

caramel chocolate brownie

- 185g (6 ounces) unsalted butter, chopped
- 200g (6½ ounces) dark (semi-sweet) chocolate, chopped coarsely
- 1½ cups (330g) caster (superfine) sugar
- 3 eggs, beaten lightly
- 1⅔ cups (250g) plain (all-purpose) flour
- ⅓ cup (35g) cocoa powder
- 200g (6½ ounces) packet jersey caramels, sliced
- cocoa powder, extra, for dusting

1 Preheat oven to 180°C/350°F. Grease a 23cm (9-inch) square slab cake pan; line base and sides with baking paper, extending paper 5cm (2 inches) above sides of pan.

2 Stir butter and chocolate in a medium saucepan over low heat until smooth.

3 Transfer mixture to a large bowl; stir in sugar and egg. Stir in sifted flour and cocoa until mixture is just combined.

4 Spread half the mixture over base of pan, top with caramels, then remaining mixture.

5 Bake about 40 minutes. Cool brownie in pan, then cut into squares. Dust with extra sifted cocoa to serve.

If you like, decorate the brownie with white chocolate curls – just run a vegetable peeler down the side of a just slightly warmed chocolate block.

makes 12
prep + cook time
1¼ hours (+ cooling)

makes 96
prep + cook time
1 hour (+ cooling)

best-ever fudge brownies

- 185g (6 ounces) unsalted butter, chopped coarsely
- 300g (9½ ounces) dark (semi-sweet) chocolate, chopped coarsely
- ¼ cup (25g) cocoa powder
- 1 cup (220g) firmly packed brown sugar
- ¾ cup (165g) caster (superfine) sugar
- 2 teaspoons vanilla extract
- 4 eggs, beaten lightly
- 1½ cups (225g) plain (all-purpose) flour
- cocoa powder, extra, for dusting

1 Preheat oven to 170°C/340°F. Grease a 20cm x 30cm (8-inch x 12-inch) rectangular pan; line base and long sides with baking paper, extending paper 2cm (¾ inch) above sides of pan.

2 Stir butter and chocolate in a medium saucepan over low heat until smooth. Remove from heat; whisk in sifted cocoa, sugars and extract until smooth. Cool slightly.

3 Stir egg and sifted flour into the chocolate mixture. Spread mixture into pan.

4 Bake about 40 minutes. Cool brownie in pan; dust with extra sifted cocoa before cutting.

tips The mixture should be barely warm when the eggs and flour are added. Use a bamboo skewer to test if the brownie is cooked; if you want a fudgy-style brownie, the skewer should feel moist; for a more cake-like brownie, bake it for a further 5 minutes or so. Store in an airtight container in the fridge for up to a week. The brownies are best served at room temperature.

dark chocolate, fig & muscat brownies

- ½ cup (100g) finely chopped dried figs
- ¼ cup (60ml) muscat
- 125g (4 ounces) butter, chopped coarsely
- 200g (6½ ounces) dark (semi-sweet) chocolate, chopped coarsely
- ⅔ cup (150g) caster (superfine) sugar
- 2 eggs, beaten lightly
- 1¼ cups (185g) plain (all-purpose) flour
- 150g (4½ ounces) dark (semi-sweet) chocolate, extra, chopped coarsely
- cocoa powder, for dusting

1 Combine figs and muscat in a small bowl; stand 20 minutes.

2 Preheat oven to 180°C/350°F. Grease a deep 19cm (8-inch) square cake pan; line base and sides with baking paper, extending paper 5cm (2 inches) above sides of pan.

3 Stir butter and chocolate in a medium saucepan over low heat until smooth. Cool for 10 minutes. Stir in sugar and egg then sifted flour, extra chocolate and the fig mixture. Spread mixture into pan.

4 Bake about 30 minutes. Cool brownie in pan. Dust with sifted cocoa, then cut into squares.

tip Dark chocolate may also be known as semi-sweet or luxury chocolate. This chocolate is made using a high percentage of cocoa liquor and cocoa butter, and may also have a little sugar added.

Tip When cocoa powder is used with other chocolate, such as in this recipe, it intensifies the chocolate flavour.

makes 36
prep + cook time
50 minutes (+ standing
& cooling)

Tip Brownie will keep in an airtight container at room temperature for 4 days; in the refrigerator for 1 week; or frozen for up to 2 months.

choc-chip brownie

- 250g (8 ounces) dark (semi-sweet) chocolate, chopped coarsely
- 150g (4½ ounces) unsalted butter, chopped coarsely
- ¼ cup (25g) cocoa powder
- 4 eggs, beaten lightly
- 1 cup (220g) firmly packed brown sugar
- ½ cup (110g) caster (superfine) sugar
- 2 teaspoons vanilla extract
- 1 cup (150g) plain (all-purpose) flour
- ½ cup (60g) ground almonds
- 100g (3 ounces) white chocolate, chopped coarsely
- 100g (3 ounces) milk chocolate, chopped coarsely
- icing (confectioners') sugar, for dusting

1 Preheat oven to 170°C/340°F. Grease a 20cm x 30cm (8-inch x 12-inch) rectangular pan; line base and sides with baking paper, extending paper 2cm (¾ inch) above sides of pan.

2 Stir dark chocolate and butter in a medium saucepan over low heat until smooth. Whisk in sifted cocoa. Transfer to a medium bowl; cool 10 minutes.

3 Whisk egg, sugars and extract into chocolate mixture, then stir in sifted flour, ground almonds and chopped white and milk chocolates.

4 Pour mixture into pan. Bake brownie for about 45 minutes. Cool cake in pan before cutting. Dust with sifted icing sugar before serving.

makes 18
prep + cook time
1¼ hours (+ cooling)

gluten-free chocolate fudge brownies

- 300g (9½ ounces) dark (semi-sweet) chocolate, chopped coarsely
- 150g (4½ ounces) butter, chopped coarsely
- 1½ cups (330g) firmly packed brown sugar
- 3 eggs, beaten lightly
- ¾ cup (75g) ground hazelnuts
- ½ cup (75g) buckwheat flour
- ½ cup (120g) sour cream
- ¼ cup (25g) cocoa powder

1 Preheat oven to 180°C/350°F. Grease 19cm x 29cm (8-inch x 12-inch) rectangular slice pan; line base and two long sides with baking paper, extending paper 2cm (¾ inch) above sides of pan.

2 Stir chocolate and butter in a medium saucepan over low heat until mixture is smooth. Add sugar; cook, stirring, for 2 minutes. Cool mixture 10 minutes.

3 Stir egg, then ground hazelnuts, flour, sour cream and 2 tablespoons of the sifted cocoa into mixture. Spread into pan.

4 Bake brownie about 45 minutes. Cool in pan then cut into squares. Dust with remaining sifted cocoa to serve.

serves 12
prep + cook time
1 hour (+ cooling)

tips Swap ground hazelnuts for ground almonds. Brownie will keep in an airtight container at room temperature for 4 days; in the refrigerator for 1 week; or frozen for up to 2 months.

fruit & nut

A favourite addition to many brownies,
fruits and nuts pair well with chocolate
- it's a match made in brownie heaven;
use your own favourite combinations.

Tips Loosely cover the blondies with foil if the almonds are browning too quickly. Store in an airtight container for up to 4 days.

christmas blondies

- ⅔ cup (220g) bottled fruit mince
- 2 tablespoons brandy
- 180g (5½ ounces) butter, softened
- 1 teaspoon vanilla extract
- 1 cup (220g) firmly packed brown sugar
- 2 eggs, beaten lightly
- 1 cup (150g) plain (all-purpose) flour
- ½ cup (75g) self-raising flour
- ½ cup (60g) ground almonds
- ½ cup (95g) white choc Bits
- 1¼ cups (100g) flaked almonds, toasted lightly
- icing (confectioners') sugar, for dusting

1 Preheat oven to 180°C/350°F. Grease a deep 20cm (8-inch) square cake pan; line base and sides with baking paper, extending paper 5cm (2 inches) above sides of pan.

2 Combine fruit mince and the brandy in a small bowl.

3 Beat butter, vanilla and sugar in a small bowl with an electric mixer until paler in colour. Add egg; beat until combined, then add sifted flours and ground almonds; beat on low speed until mixture is combined.

4 Stir fruit mince mixture, chocolate and half the nuts into mixture. Spread mixture into pan; sprinkle with remaining nuts.

5 Bake for 40 minutes or until a skewer inserted into the centre comes out with a few crumbs attached (but not wet blondie batter).

6 Cool brownie in pan before cutting into squares. Dust with sifted icing sugar before serving.

makes 16
prep + cook time
1 hour (+ cooling)

makes 24
prep + cook time
1¼ hours (+ cooling)

date & almond brownies

- 300g (9½ ounces) dark (semi-sweet) chocolate, chopped coarsely
- 200g (6½ ounces) butter, chopped coarsely
- 125g (4 ounces) fresh dates, seeded
- 4 eggs, beaten lightly
- ¾ cup (165g) caster (superfine) sugar
- 1 cup (120g) ground almonds
- ⅔ cup (100g) plain (all-purpose) flour
- 1 tablespoon cocoa powder
- 2 tablespoons toasted flaked almonds
- cocoa powder, extra, for dusting

1 Preheat oven to 170°C/340°F. Grease a deep 23cm (9-inch) square cake pan; line base and sides with baking paper, extending paper 5cm (2 inches) above sides.

2 Stir chocolate and butter in a medium saucepan over low heat until smooth. Stir in dates. Transfer mixture to a medium bowl; cool 10 minutes.

3 Whisk egg and sugar into chocolate mixture. Stir in ground almonds, and sifted flour and cocoa. Pour mixture into pan; sprinkle with nuts.

4 Bake about 35 minutes. Cool brownies in pan before cutting. Dust with a little extra sifted cocoa powder before serving.

hazelnut brownies

- **125g (4 ounces) butter**
- **200g (6½ ounces) dark (semi-sweet) chocolate, chopped coarsely**
- **½ cup (110g) caster (superfine) sugar**
- **2 eggs, beaten lightly**
- **1¼ cups (185g) plain (all-purpose) flour**
- **½ cup (70g) toasted hazelnuts, chopped coarsely**
- **1 cup (190g) white choc Bits**

1 Preheat oven to 180°C/350°F. Grease a deep 19cm (8-inch) square cake pan; line base and two opposite sides with baking paper, extending paper 5cm (2 inches) above sides.

2 Stir butter and chocolate in a medium saucepan over low heat until smooth. Stir in sugar; cook, stirring, 5 minutes. Cool 10 minutes.

3 Stir eggs and flour then nuts and choc Bits into chocolate mixture. Spread mixture into pan.

4 Bake about 30 minutes. Cool brownie in pan; cut when cold.

tip The hazelnut, also known as filbert, is a plump, grape-sized, rich, sweet nut. It has a brown inedible skin that is removed by rubbing heated nuts together vigorously in a clean tea towel.

serves 12
prep + cook time
50 minutes (+ cooling)

Tip Brownie will keep in an airtight container at room temperature for 4 days; in the refrigerator for 1 week; or frozen for up to 2 months.

Tip This recipe can be made a week ahead; keep in an airtight container in the refrigerator.

fudgy choc-nut brownies

- 125g (4 ounces) butter, chopped
- 90g (3 ounces) dark (semi-sweet) chocolate, chopped coarsely
- 90g (3 ounces) milk chocolate, chopped coarsely
- ½ cup (110g) firmly packed brown sugar
- 2 tablespoons honey
- 2 eggs, beaten lightly
- 1 cup (150g) plain (all-purpose) flour
- ⅔ cup (100g) macadamia nuts, chopped coarsely

1 Preheat oven to 180°C/350°F. Grease a deep 19cm (8-inch) square cake pan; line base and two opposite sides with baking paper, extending paper 5cm (2 inches) above sides.
2 Stir butter and chocolates in a medium saucepan over low heat until smooth. Remove from heat; stir in sugar and honey. Stir in egg, then sifted flour and nuts; pour mixture into pan.
3 Bake about 30 minutes. Cool brownie in pan; cut when cold.

tip Macadamia nuts, also known as 'bush nuts' are native to Australia. This rich, buttery nut is found inside an extremely hard to crack shell. Because of their high oil content they should be stored in the refrigerator.

makes 12
prep + cook time
50 minutes (+ cooling)

white chocolate, nut & berry blondies

- 125g (4 ounces) butter, chopped coarsely
- 300g (9½ ounces) white chocolate, chopped coarsely
- ¾ cup (165g) caster (superfine) sugar
- 2 eggs, beaten lightly
- ¾ cup (110g) plain (all-purpose) flour
- ½ cup (75g) self-raising flour
- ½ cup (75g) coarsely chopped toasted macadamias
- 150g (4½ ounces) fresh or frozen raspberries

1 Preheat oven to 180°C/350°F. Grease a 23cm (9-inch) square slab cake pan; line base and sides with baking paper, extending paper 2cm (¾ inch) above sides.

2 Stir butter and two-thirds of the chocolate in a medium saucepan over low heat until smooth. Cool 10 minutes.

3 Whisk sugar and egg into chocolate mixture. Stir in sifted flours, nuts, berries and remaining chocolate. Spread mixture into pan.

4 Bake about 40 minutes. Cool blondie in pan; cut when cold.

makes 25
prep + cook
1¼ hours (+ cooling)

Tip Blondies will keep in an airtight container at room temperature for 1 day; in the refrigerator for 2 days; or frozen for up to 2 months.

tip Blondie will keep in an airtight container at room temperature for 1 day, or in the refrigerator for 2 days.

caramelised apple blondie

- 4 medium apples (600g)
- 50g (1½ ounces) butter
- ½ cup (110g) caster (superfine) sugar
- 300g (9½ ounces) white chocolate
- 90g (3 ounces) butter, extra
- ½ cup (110g) caster (superfine) sugar, extra
- 1½ cups (225g) self-raising flour
- 3 eggs, beaten lightly

serves 12
prep + cook time
1¼ hours

1 Preheat oven to 160°C/325°F. Grease a closed 24cm/9½-inch (base measurement) springform pan; line base and side with baking paper.

2 Peel, halve and core apples; cut each half into 8 wedges. Melt butter with sugar in a large frying pan; stir over medium heat until caramelised. Add apple to butter mixture; cook, turning occasionally, for 8 minutes or until apples are soft.

3 Carefully remove apples from caramel; place around the outside edge of pan. Reserve remaining caramel.

4 Meanwhile, break chocolate into a medium saucepan, add extra butter; stir over low heat until smooth. Remove from heat; stir in extra sugar until combined. Cool for 10 minutes or until mixture is just warm.

5 Stir sifted flour and egg into mixture. Spread mixture over apples. Bake about 50 minutes.

6 Reheat reserved caramel. Turn blondie onto a serving plate; serve with caramel, and cream, if you like.

Tip Store in an airtight container for up to 4 days.

rocky road brownie slice

- ⅓ cup (25g) desiccated coconut
- 100g (3 ounces) butter, chopped coarsely
- 200g (6½ ounces) dark (semi-sweet) chocolate, chopped coarsely
- 1 cup (220g) firmly packed brown sugar
- 2 eggs, beaten lightly
- ½ cup (75g) plain (all-purpose) flour
- ⅓ cup (80g) sour cream
- 300g (9½ ounces) white chocolate
- 200g (6½ ounces) marshmallows
- ½ cup (70g) toasted slivered almonds, chopped coarsely

1 Preheat oven to 180°C/350°F. Grease a 20cm x 30cm (8-inch x 12-inch) rectangular slice pan; line base and long sides with baking paper, extending paper 5cm (2 inches) above sides.

2 Place coconut in a small ovenproof dish; brown, in oven, stirring frequently, for 2 minutes or until coconut is lightly golden, cool. (This can be done under a medium-hot grill/broiler, if you like.)

3 Stir butter and dark chocolate in a medium saucepan over low heat until smooth. Cool for 10 minutes.

4 Stir sugar and egg into chocolate mixture, then stir in sifted flour and sour cream. Spread mixture into pan.

5 Bake about 35 minutes; cool brownie in pan.

6 Melt white chocolate in a medium heatproof bowl over a medium saucepan of simmering water (don't let water touch base of bowl).

7 Chop marshmallows coarsely; combine with nuts and coconut in a medium bowl, then sprinkle over brownie slice. Drizzle with white chocolate. Refrigerate to set before cutting.

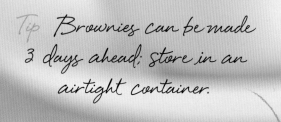

Tip Brownies can be made 3 days ahead; store in an airtight container.

pecan and chocolate brownies

- 80g (2½ ounces) butter, chopped coarsely
- 150g (4½ ounces) dark (semi-sweet) chocolate, chopped coarsely
- ¾ cup (165g) firmly packed brown sugar
- 2 eggs, beaten lightly
- 1 teaspoon vanilla extract
- ⅔ cup (100g) plain (all-purpose) flour
- 1 tablespoon cocoa powder
- 50g (1½ ounces) dark (semi-sweet) chocolate, chopped coarsely, extra
- ¼ cup (30g) coarsely chopped pecans

1 Preheat oven to 200°C/400°F. Grease eight holes of a 12-hole (⅓-cup/80ml) muffin pan; line bases with rounds of baking paper.

2 Combine butter, chocolate and sugar in a medium heavy-based saucepan; stir over low heat until smooth. Transfer mixture to a large bowl; cool 10 minutes.

3 Stir egg, extract, sifted flour and cocoa into chocolate mixture; stir in extra chocolate. Divide mixture evenly into prepared pan holes; sprinkle with nuts.

4 Bake about 20 minutes. Stand muffins in pan for 5 minutes before turning, top-side up, onto a wire rack to cool.

makes 8
prep + cook time
40 minutes (+ cooling)

makes 40
prep + cook time
40 minutes (+ cooling)

double chocolate
& raspberry brownies

- 275g (9 ounces) dark (semi-sweet) chocolate, chopped coarsely
- 155g (5 ounces) butter, chopped coarsely
- 1½ cups (330g) caster (superfine) sugar
- 3 eggs, beaten lightly
- 1½ cups (225g) plain (all-purpose) flour
- 155g (5 ounces) frozen raspberries
- 155g (5 ounces) white chocolate, chopped coarsely

1 Preheat oven to 180°C/350°F. Grease a 20cm x 30cm (8-inch x 12-inch) rectangular pan; line base and long sides with baking paper, extending paper 2cm (¾ inch) above sides.

2 Stir dark chocolate and butter in a large heatproof bowl over a large saucepan of simmering water until smooth (don't let water touch base of bowl); stir in sugar.

3 Remove from heat; cool 10 minutes. Stir in egg, sifted flour, raspberries and white chocolate.

4 Spread mixture into pan. Bake for 25 minutes. Cool brownie in pan; cut when cold.

Tips Use the raspberries while they are still frozen for best results. Store in an airtight container for up to 3 days.

Tips If using frozen raspberries, don't thaw them before adding to the mixture, otherwise they'll bleed and won't retain their shape. Store in an airtight container in the refrigerator for up to 4 days.

chocolate raspberry brownies

- 150g (4½ ounces) butter, chopped coarsely
- 350g (11 ounces) dark (semi-sweet) chocolate, chopped coarsely
- 1 cup (220g) caster (superfine) sugar
- 2 eggs, beaten lightly
- 1¼ cups (185g) plain (all-purpose) flour
- ½ cup (75g) self-raising flour
- 200g (6½ ounces) fresh or frozen raspberries
- cocoa powder, for dusting

1 Preheat oven to 180°C/350°F. Grease a deep 20cm (8-inch) square cake pan; line base and sides with baking paper, extending paper 5cm (2 inches) above sides.

2 Stir butter and 200g (6½ ounces) of the chocolate in a medium saucepan over low heat until smooth. Cool for 10 minutes.

3 Stir sugar, egg, sifted flours, raspberries and remaining chopped chocolate into chocolate mixture; spread into pan.

4 Bake about 45 minutes. Cool brownie in pan; cut when cold. Serve brownies dusted with sifted cocoa.

makes 16
prep + cook time
1¼ hours (+ cooling)

cherry coconut brownies

- 125g (4 ounces) butter, chopped coarsely
- 200g (6½ ounces) dark (semi-sweet) chocolate, chopped coarsely
- 1 cup (220g) caster (superfine) sugar
- ¾ cup (110g) plain (all-purpose) flour
- ¼ cup (35g) self-raising flour
- 2 tablespoons cocoa powder
- 2 eggs, beaten lightly
- ¼ cup (20g) desiccated coconut
- 1 x 80g (2½-ounce) Cherry Ripe chocolate bar, chopped coarsely
- cocoa powder, extra for dusting

1 Preheat oven to 180°C/350°F. Grease a 23cm (9-inch) square slab cake pan; line base and two opposite sides with baking paper, extending paper 5cm (2 inches) over sides.

2 Stir butter and chocolate in a medium saucepan over low heat until smooth. Cool mixture until just warm.

3 Stir sugar, combined sifted flours and cocoa, egg, coconut and half the Cherry Ripe into chocolate mixture. Spread mixture into pan; top with remaining Cherry Ripe.

4 Bake about 40 minutes. Cool brownie in pan; cut when cold. Dust brownies with sifted extra cocoa before serving.

makes 24
prep + cook time
1 hour (+ cooling)

Tip Store in an airtight container for up to 4 days.

Tips These treats are best served while still warm. Rolos are round caramel-filled chocolates.

walnut brownie bites

- ½ cup (50g) walnuts, toasted, chopped finely
- 80g (2½ ounces) butter
- 150g (4½ ounces) dark (semi-sweet) chocolate, chopped coarsely
- ¾ cup (150g) firmly packed brown sugar
- 1 egg, beaten lightly
- ⅓ cup (50g) plain (all-purpose) flour
- ¼ cup (60g) sour cream
- 3 x 50g (1½-ounce) packets Rolos

1 Preheat oven to 180°C/350°F. Lightly grease two non-stick 12-hole (1½-tablespoon) mini muffin pans; divide walnuts among holes.

2 Stir butter and chocolate in a small saucepan over low heat until smooth. Stir in sugar. Cool mixture until just warm.

3 Stir egg, then sifted flour, and sour cream into mixture; spoon mixture into pan holes. Press one Rolo into centre of mixture in each pan hole; spread mixture so Rolo is completely covered.

4 Bake about 15 minutes. Using a sharp-pointed knife, loosen sides of brownies from pan; stand in pan for 10 minutes before gently removing. Serve brownies warm.

makes 24
prep + cook time
40 minutes (+ standing)

Tip Store in an airtight container for up to 4 days.

peanut butter brownies

- 180g (5½ ounces) butter, chopped coarsely
- 150g (4½ ounces) dark (semi-sweet) chocolate, chopped coarsely
- 1¾ cups (385g) caster (superfine) sugar
- 4 eggs, beaten lightly
- 1 teaspoon vanilla extract
- ¾ cup (110g) plain (all-purpose) flour
- 2 tablespoons self-raising flour
- ⅓ cup (35g) cocoa powder
- 50g (1½ ounces) dark (semi-sweet) chocolate, chopped coarsely, extra
- ⅓ cup (95g) crunchy peanut butter

1 Preheat oven to 160°C/325°F. Grease a 20cm x 30cm (8-inch x 12-inch) rectangular slice pan; line base and two long sides with baking paper, extending paper 2cm (¾ inch) above sides.

2 Stir butter and chocolate in a medium saucepan over low heat until smooth; cool for 10 minutes or until mixture is just warm.

3 Stir sugar, egg and extract into chocolate mixture, then stir in sifted flours and cocoa, then extra chocolate.

4 Pour mixture into pan. Drop small spoonfuls of peanut butter onto the chocolate mixture; swirl through the mixture with a knife.

5 Bake about 50 minutes or until firm. Cool brownie in pan; cut when cold.

makes 24
prep + cook time
1½ hours (+ cooling)

dessert

A fudgy chocolate brownie served with rich, creamy ice-cream and accompanied with warm chocolate or caramel sauce — or both — is the perfect dessert.

tips The sauce can be made a day ahead; store, covered, in the refrigerator. Gently reheat before serving. Store brownie in an airtight container for up to 4 days.

chocolate brownies
with chocolate sauce

- **150g (4½ ounces) butter, chopped coarsely**
- **300g (9½ ounces) dark (semi-sweet) chocolate, chopped coarsely**
- **1½ cups (330g) firmly packed brown sugar**
- **4 eggs, beaten lightly**
- **1 cup (150g) plain (all-purpose) flour**
- **½ cup (120g) sour cream**
- **½ cup (60g) toasted hazelnuts, chopped coarsely**

chocolate sauce

- **150g (4½ ounces) dark (semi-sweet) chocolate, chopped coarsely**
- **1 cup (250ml) pouring cream**
- **⅓ cup (75g) firmly packed brown sugar**
- **2 teaspoons hazelnut-flavoured liqueur**

1 Preheat oven to 180°C/350°F. Grease a 20cm x 30cm (8-inch x 12-inch) rectangular slice pan; line base and two long sides with baking paper, extending paper 2cm (¾ inch) over sides.

2 Stir butter and chocolate in a medium saucepan over low heat until smooth. Transfer mixture to a medium bowl; cool 10 minutes.

3 Stir in sugar and egg, then sifted flour, sour cream and nuts. Spread mixture into pan.

4 Bake about 30 minutes.

5 Meanwhile, make chocolate sauce.

6 Cut warm brownie into 16 pieces. Serve brownies drizzled with warm sauce. Accompany with vanilla or coffee ice-cream, if you like.

chocolate sauce Stir chocolate, cream and sugar in a small saucepan over low heat until mixture is smooth. Simmer, uncovered, for 1 minute. Remove from heat; stir in liqueur.

serves 8
prep + cook time
50 minutes (+ cooling)

cheesecake brownies

- 125g (4 ounces) butter, chopped coarsely
- 150g (4½ ounces) dark (semi-sweet) chocolate, chopped coarsely
- 1 egg
- ⅔ cup (150g) caster (superfine) sugar
- ¾ cup (110g) plain (all-purpose) flour
- ¼ cup (35g) self-raising flour

cream cheese topping

- 250g (8 ounces) cream cheese, softened
- 1 teaspoon vanilla extract
- ⅓ cup (75g) caster (superfine) sugar
- 1 egg
- ½ cup (125ml) pouring cream

1 Preheat oven to 180°C/350°F. Grease a deep 19cm (8-inch) square cake pan; line base and sides with baking paper, extending paper 5cm (2 inches) above sides of pan.

2 Stir butter and chocolate in a small saucepan over low heat until smooth; cool.

3 Beat egg and sugar in a small bowl with an electric mixer until thick and creamy. Stir in chocolate mixture and sifted flours. Spread mixture into pan; bake about 10 minutes.

4 Meanwhile, make cream cheese topping; pour over brownie base.

5 Bake cheesecake for 15 minutes or until just set. Cool in oven with door ajar. Refrigerate 3 hours before serving.

cream cheese topping
Beat cream cheese, extract, sugar and egg in a small bowl with an electric mixer until smooth; beat in cream.

makes 16
prep + cook time
1 hour (+ cooling & refrigeration)

Tips This versatile slice can be served cut (straight from the fridge) into small finger-lengths as a treat or, cut into squares and topped with fresh berries for a charming dessert. For a more tart flavour, drizzle over some passionfruit pulp.

tip Brownie will keep in an airtight container at room temperature for 4 days; in the refrigerator for 1 week; or frozen for up to 2 months.

chocolate brownies

- 30g (1 ounce) unsalted butter, chopped
- 250g (8 ounces) dark (semi-sweet) chocolate, chopped coarsely
- 80g (2½ ounces) unsalted butter, extra, softened
- 2 teaspoons vanilla extract
- 1 cup (220g) firmly packed brown sugar
- 2 eggs
- ½ cup (75g) plain (all-purpose) flour
- ½ cup (70g) coarsely chopped toasted hazelnuts
- ⅓ cup (80g) sour cream, softened

chocolate icing

- 125g (4 ounces) dark (semi-sweet) chocolate, chopped coarsely
- 60g (2 ounces) unsalted butter, chopped

1 Preheat oven to 180°C/350°F. Grease a deep 19cm (8-inch) square cake pan; line base and sides with baking paper, extending paper 5cm (2 inches) above sides of pan.

2 Stir chopped butter and chocolate in a small saucepan over low heat until smooth. Cool mixture 5 minutes.

3 Beat softened butter, vanilla and sugar in a small bowl with an electric mixer until light and fluffy. Beat in eggs, one at a time, until combined.

4 Transfer mixture to a large bowl. Stir in sifted flour, chocolate mixture, nuts and sour cream.

5 Spread mixture into pan. Bake about 45 minutes; cool brownie in pan.

6 Make chocolate icing.

7 Turn brownie, top-side up, onto a wire rack; spread with icing. Cut into squares to serve.

chocolate icing Melt chocolate and butter in a small heatproof bowl over a small saucepan of simmering water (do not allow water to touch base of bowl). Remove bowl from heat; cool to room temperature. Beat with a wooden spoon until icing is thick and spreadable.

makes 20
prep + cook time
1¼ hours (+ cooling)

black forest brownies with cherry ganache

- ½ cup (100g) bottled amarena cherries in syrup (reserve syrup for ganache)
- 125g (4 ounces) butter, chopped
- 185g (6 ounces) dark (semi-sweet) chocolate, chopped coarsely
- 1 cup (220g) caster (superfine) sugar
- ¼ cup (60ml) water
- 2 eggs, beaten lightly
- 1 cup (150g) plain (all-purpose) flour
- 24 fresh cherries (175g)

cherry ganache

- ½ cup (125m) pouring cream
- ⅓ cup (80ml) amarena cherry syrup (from the reserved syrup, above)
- 220g (7 ounces) dark (semi-sweet) chocolate, chopped coarsely

1 Preheat oven to 180°C/350°F. Grease a 20cm x 30cm (8-inch x 12-inch) rectangular slice pan; line base and two long sides with baking paper, extending paper 2cm (¾ inch) above sides.

2 Drain cherries, reserving syrup for the cherry chocolate ganache. Chop cherries coarsely.

3 Stir butter and chocolate in a small saucepan over low heat until smooth. Transfer to a large bowl; cool for 10 minutes.

4 Stir sugar and the water, then egg, sifted flour and amarena cherries into chocolate mixture; pour into pan.

5 Bake about 30 minutes or until set; cool brownie in pan.

6 Meanwhile, make cherry ganache.

7 Turn brownie, top-side up, onto a serving plate. Spread cherry ganache over brownie; cut into 24 pieces. Top each piece with a fresh cherry to serve.

cherry ganache Heat cream and syrup in a small saucepan until almost boiling, add chocolate; whisk until smooth. Refrigerate for 1 hour or until ganache is of a spreadable consistency.

Tip Amarena cherries are small sour cherries; they are available in syrup from speciality Italian delis.

makes 24
prep + cook time 1 hour
(+ standing & refrigeration)

Tips Assemble cake just before serving. Ice-cream can be made a week ahead. Brownie can be made 2 days ahead.

raspberry brownie ice-cream cake

- 1 litre (4 cups) vanilla ice-cream, softened
- 150g (4½ ounces) frozen raspberries
- 125g (4 ounces) butter, chopped coarsely
- 200g (6½ ounces) dark (semi-sweet) chocolate, chopped coarsely
- ½ cup (110g) caster (superfine) sugar
- 2 eggs, beaten lightly
- 1¼ cups (185g) plain (all-purpose) flour
- 150g (4½ ounces) milk chocolate, chopped coarsely
- icing (confectioners') sugar, for dusting

1 Line a deep 23cm (9-inch) round cake pan with plastic wrap, extending wrap so it will cover pan.

2 Combine ice-cream and raspberries in a medium bowl. Spoon ice-cream into pan; smooth surface. Fold plastic wrap over to enclose ice-cream. Freeze 3 hours or until firm.

3 Once firm, remove ice-cream from pan, still wrapped in plastic; place on tray. Return to freezer.

4 Preheat oven to 160°C/1325°F.

5 Grease same cake pan; line base and side with baking paper.

6 Stir butter, dark chocolate and sugar in a medium saucepan over low heat until smooth. Cool 10 minutes.

7 Stir egg, sifted flour and milk chocolate into chocolate mixture. Spread mixture into pan.

8 Bake about 30 minutes; cool brownie in pan.

9 Split brownie in half. Sandwich ice-cream cake between brownie rounds; dust with sifted icing sugar and serve immediately. Top with fresh raspberries, if you like.

serves 12
prep + cook time 1 hour
(+ freezing & cooling)

brownie ice-cream stacks

- 500ml (2 cups) vanilla ice-cream, softened
- 80g (2½ ounces) butter, chopped coarsely
- 150g (4½ ounces) dark (semi-sweet) chocolate, chopped coarsely
- ¾ cup (150g) firmly packed brown sugar
- 2 eggs, beaten lightly
- ½ cup (75g) plain (all-purpose) flour
- ¼ cup (60g) sour cream
- ½ cup (50g) coarsely chopped walnuts

hot fudge sauce
- 50g (2 ounces) dark (semi-sweet) chocolate, chopped coarsely
- ½ cup (125ml) pouring cream
- 2 tablespoons brown sugar
- ½ teaspoon instant coffee granules
- 1 tablespoon coffee-flavoured liqueur

1 Line base and sides of an 8cm x 26cm (3¼-inch x 10½-inch) bar cake pan with baking paper. Press ice-cream into pan, cover with foil; freeze overnight.
2 Preheat oven to 180°C/350°F. Line base and sides of another 8cm x 26cm (3¼-inch x 10½-inch) bar cake pan with baking paper.
3 Stir butter and chocolate in a medium saucepan over low heat until smooth. Cool until just warm.
4 Stir sugar, egg, sifted flour, sour cream and nuts into chocolate mixture. Spread mixture into pan.
5 Bake about 40 minutes Cool brownie in pan.

6 Meanwhile, make hot fudge sauce.
7 Turn brownie onto board; remove paper. Trim narrow ends; cut brownie into 12 slices.
8 Turn ice-cream out of pan; cut into eight slices. Stack alternate slices of ice-cream and brownie, starting and finishing with a brownie. Drizzle stacks with hot fudge sauce.

hot fudge sauce Stir chocolate, cream, sugar and coffee in a small saucepan over low heat until mixture is smooth. Bring to a boil; reduce heat, simmer, uncovered, for 2 minutes. Remove from heat; stir in liqueur.

serves 4
prep + cook time
1½ hours (+ freezing & cooling)

Tip Brownie can be made
4 days ahead; store in
an airtight container.

AMARENA CHERRIES IN SYRUP small sour cherries preserved in sugar syrup to retain their natural garnet colour and cherry taste. They are available from speciality delis and good greengrocers.

BAKING PAPER also known as parchment paper or baking parchment – is a silicone-coated paper that is primarily used for lining baking pans and oven trays so cakes and biscuits won't stick, making removal easy.

BAKING POWDER a raising agent consisting mainly of two parts cream of tartar to one part bicarbonate of soda.

BICARBONATE OF SODA (BAKING SODA) an acid and alkaline combination, which when moistened and heated, gives off carbon dioxide that aerates and lightens the mixture during baking.

BUTTER 125g is equal to one stick (4 ounces) of butter.

unsalted butter, often called 'sweet' butter; simply has no added salt. It is mainly used in baking, and if the recipe calls for unsalted butter, it should not be substituted.

CHEESE

cream commonly known as Philadelphia or Philly, a soft cows'-milk cheese with a fat content of at least 33%. Sold at supermarkets.

mascarpone a fresh, unripened, smooth, triple cream cheese made in much the same way as yoghurt. Has a rich, sweet, slightly acidic taste.

CHOCOLATE

Cherry Ripe a confectionery bar containing a mix of coconut and cherries that is covered in thick chocolate.

choc Bits also known as chocolate chips and chocolate morsels; available in milk, white and dark chocolate. Made of cocoa liquor, cocoa butter, sugar and an emulsifier; they hold their shape in baking and are ideal for decorating.

chocolate hazelnut spread we use Nutella; developed during World War II when chocolate was in short supply, hazelnuts were added to extend the chocolate.

dark also known as semi-sweet or luxury chocolate; made of a high percentage of cocoa liquor and cocoa butter, and a little added sugar. Unless stated, we use dark chocolate in this book.

Melts small discs of compound milk, white or dark chocolate; it is ideal for melting and moulding as it holds its shape well. Available as dark, milk and white chocolate.

milk most popular eating chocolate, mild and very sweet; similar in make-up to dark with the difference being the addition of milk solids.

mint patties a soft, round mint fondant confectionery covered with chocolate.

Rolos a brand of bucket-shaped chocolates with a soft runny caramel centre (although, in the UK and US, the filling is thicker and more chewy).

white contains no cocoa solids but derives its sweet flavour from cocoa butter. Very sensitive to heat so watch carefully if melting.

COCOA POWDER also known as cocoa; dried, unsweetened, roasted then ground cocoa beans (cacao seeds).

dutch cocoa is treated with an alkali to neutralize its acids. It has a reddish-brown colour, mild flavour, and is easy to dissolve in liquids.

COCONUT

desiccated unsweetened, dried, very finely shredded coconut.

shredded unsweetened thin strips of dried coconut flesh.

CRANBERRIES, DRIED have a rich, astringent flavour and can be used in both sweet and savoury dishes. Can usually be substituted for or with other dried fruit.

CREAM we used fresh cream, also known as pure or pouring cream unless otherwise stated. It contains no additives and has a minimum fat content of 35 per cent.

sour a thick commercially cultured soured cream with a minimum fat content of 35 per cent.

thick (double) a dolloping cream with a minimum fat content of 45 per cent.

thickened (heavy) a whipping cream containing a thickener. Has a minimum fat content of 35 per cent.

CURRANTS, DRIED tiny, almost black-coloured raisins.

glossary

CUSTARD POWDER instant powdered mixture used to make pouring custard; similar to North American instant pudding mixes.

DAIRY FREE

tofutti 'better than cream cheese' is a tofu-based dairy-free cream cheese substitute, available in the fridge section of supermarkets and health-food stores.

dark chocolate choose a dark chocolate that has no added milk or other dairy ingredients.

dairy-free spread we used Diet Becel, a commercial product having a fat content of 2.4g fat per 5g of spread.

DATES fruit of the date palm tree, eaten fresh or dried. About 4cm to 6cm in length, oval and plump, thin-skinned, with a honey-sweet flavour and sticky texture.

EGGS some recipes in this book may call for raw or barely cooked eggs; exercise caution if there is a salmonella problem in your area. The risk is greater for those who are pregnant, elderly or very young, and those with impaired immune systems.

EXTRACT/ESSENCE essence is an artificial creation of a food flavour. An extract is made by extracting the flavour from a food product. Essences and extracts keep indefinitely if stored in a cool dark place.

FLOUR

buckwheat a herb in the same plant family as rhubarb; not a cereal so it is gluten-free.

gluten-free plain a blend of corn, potato and tapioca starches and rice flour.

gluten-free self raising similar to gluten-free plain flour but with the addition of a raising agent (usually baking powder).

plain a general (all-purpose) flour made from wheat.

self-raising (rising) plain or wholemeal plain flour that has been combined with baking powder in the proportion of 1 cup flour to 2 teaspoons baking powder.

tapioca a starch extracted from the root of the tropical cassava plant.

FRUIT MINCE also known as mincemeat. A mixture of dried fruits, such as raisins, sultanas, apple and candied peel and nuts, spices, brandy or rum. Is used as a filling for fruit mince pies, cakes and puddings.

GLACE CHERRIES or candied cherries; boiled in a heavy sugar syrup then dried.

GLACE GINGER fresh ginger root preserved in sugar syrup.

JAM also known as preserve or conserve.

JERSEY CARAMELS two layers of sweetened condensed milk caramel sandwiching a layer of white fondant. A chewy and sweet confection.

LIQUEUR

coffee-flavoured use Kahlúa, Tia Maria or your favourite coffee-flavoured liqueur.

hazelnut-flavoured use Frangelico or your favourite hazelnut-flavoured liqueur.

LOLLIES a confectionery also known as sweets or candy.

MARMALADE a preserve, usually based on citrus fruit.

MARSHMALLOW a light, airy confectionery that holds its shape. Made from glucose, sugar, gelatine and cornflour.

MIXED DRIED FRUIT a combination of sultanas, raisins, currants, mixed peel and cherries.

MIXED SPICE a classic spice mixture generally containing caraway, allspice, coriander, cumin, nutmeg and ginger, although cinnamon and other spices can be added. It is used with fruit and in cakes.

MUSCAT is a sweet, fruity dessert wine; made from the grape of the same name, and is almost caramel in colour.

NUTMEG a strong, pungent spice ground from the dried nut of an evergreen tree native to Indonesia. Usually found ground but the flavour is more intense from a whole nut, available from spice shops, so it's best to grate your own.

NUTS

almonds flat, pointy-ended nuts with pitted brown shells enclosing a brown skin, underneath which lies a creamy white kernel.

flaked paper-thin slices.

ground also known as almond meal; nuts are powdered to a coarse flour-like texture.

slivered small lengthways-cut pieces.

brazil a triangular white-fleshed nut with a hard brown shell.

cashew a kidney-shaped nut that grows out from the bottom of the cashew apple. They have a sweet, buttery flavour and contain about 48 per cent fat. Because of their high fat content, they should be stored, tightly wrapped, in the refrigerator.

hazelnuts also known as filberts; plump, grape-sized, rich, sweet nut.

ground also known as hazelnut meal. Nuts are powdered to a coarse flour-like texture.

macadamia a rich, buttery nut native to Australia; stored in the refrigerator because of its high oil content.

pecans a golden-brown, rich, buttery nut.

pine also known as pignoli; not in fact a nut but a small, cream-coloured kernel from pine cones.

pistachios pale green, delicately flavoured nuts inside hard off-white shells. *To peel*, soak shelled nuts in boiling water for about 5 minutes; drain, then pat dry with absorbent paper. Rub skins with a clean cloth to peel.

walnut the kernel forms into two distinct halves; it has a white flesh with a light brown skin. They are high in protein and essential fatty acids.

NUTS, ROASTING spread shelled, peeled nuts, in a single layer, on an oven tray; roast in a 160°C/325°F oven, stirring frequently, for 8 to 10 minutes. Be careful to avoid burning nuts.

NUTS, TOASTING place shelled, peeled nuts, in a single layer, in a small dry frying pan; cook, stirring constantly, over low heat, until fragrant and just changed in colour. Remove immediately from pan to stop burning.

PEANUT BUTTER peanuts are ground to a paste; available in crunchy and smooth varieties.

POLENTA also known as cornmeal; a flour-like cereal made of dried corn (maize). Also the dish made from it.

RAISINS dried sweet grapes (traditionally muscatel grapes).

RHUBARB has thick, celery-like stalks that can reach up to 60cm long; the stalks are the only edible portion of the plant – the leaves contain a toxic substance.

ROLLED OATS flattened oat grain rolled into flakes and traditionally used for porridge. Instant oats are also available, but we prefer to use traditional oats for baking.

STAR ANISE dried star-shaped pod with seeds having an astringent aniseed flavour. Available whole and ground, it is a part of five-spice powder.

SWEETENED CONDENSED MILK a canned milk product from which 60% of the water has been removed; the remaining milk is then sweetened with sugar.

SUGAR

brown an extremely soft, fine granulated sugar retaining molasses for its characteristic colour and flavour.

caster also known as superfine or finely granulated table sugar. Dissolves more quickly than white (granulated) sugar due to its smaller grain size.

demerara a small-grained golden-coloured crystal sugar.

icing also confectioners' sugar or powdered sugar; is white (granulated) sugar crushed together with a small amount of added cornflour.

icing, pure also known as confectioners' sugar or powdered sugar, but has no added cornflour.

raw natural brown granulated sugar.

white a coarse, granulated table sugar, also known as crystal sugar.

SYRUP

golden a concentrated, refined sugar syrup with a distinctive flavour and golden colour. Pure maple syrup can be substituted, if necessary.

treacle a concentrated, refined sugar syrup with a distinctive flavour and dark black colour.

VANILLA BEAN dried, long, thin pod from a tropical golden orchid; the tiny black seeds are used to impart a vanilla flavour in baking and desserts. Place a whole bean in a jar of sugar to make the vanilla sugar often called for in recipes; a bean can be used three or four times.

extract made by extracting the flavour from the vanilla bean pod; the pods are soaked, usually in alcohol, to capture the authentic flavour.

conversion chart

measures

One Australian metric measuring cup holds approximately 250ml, one Australian metric tablespoon holds 20ml, one Australian metric teaspoon holds 5ml. The difference between one country's measuring cups and another's is within a 2- or 3-teaspoon variance, and will not affect your cooking results. North America, New Zealand and the United Kingdom use a 15ml tablespoon. All cup and spoon measurements are level. The most accurate way of measuring dry ingredients is to weigh them. When measuring liquids, use a clear glass or plastic jug with metric markings. We use large eggs with an average weight of 60g.

dry measures

METRIC	IMPERIAL
15g	½oz
30g	1oz
60g	2oz
90g	3oz
125g	4oz (¼lb)
155g	5oz
185g	6oz
220g	7oz
250g	8oz (½lb)
280g	9oz
315g	10oz
345g	11oz
375g	12oz (¾lb)
410g	13oz
440g	14oz
470g	15oz
500g	16oz (1lb)
750g	24oz (1½lb)
1kg	32oz (2lb)

liquid measures

METRIC	IMPERIAL
30ml	1 fluid oz
60ml	2 fluid oz
100ml	3 fluid oz
125ml	4 fluid oz
150ml	5 fluid oz
190ml	6 fluid oz
250ml	8 fluid oz
300ml	10 fluid oz
500ml	16 fluid oz
600ml	20 fluid oz
1000ml (1 litre)	1¾ pints

length measures

METRIC	IMPERIAL
3mm	⅛in
6mm	¼in
1cm	½in
2cm	¾in
2.5cm	1in
5cm	2in
6cm	2½in
8cm	3in
10cm	4in
13cm	5in
15cm	6in
18cm	7in
20cm	8in
23cm	9in
25cm	10in
28cm	11in
30cm	12in (1ft)

oven temperatures

These oven temperatures are only a guide for conventional ovens. For fan-forced ovens, check the manufacturer's manual.

	°C (CELSIUS)	°F (FAHRENHEIT)
Very slow	120	250
Slow	150	275-300
Moderately slow	160	325
Moderate	180	350-375
Moderately hot	200	400
Hot	220	425-450
Very hot	240	475

The imperial measurements used in these recipes are approximate only. Measurements for cake pans are approximate only. Using same-shaped cake pans of a similar size should not affect the outcome of your baking. We measure the inside top of the cake pan to determine sizes.

Published in 2014 by Bauer Media Books, Sydney
Bauer Media Books are published by Bauer Media Limited
54 Park St, Sydney
GPO Box 4088, Sydney, NSW 2001.
phone (02) 9282 8618; fax (02) 9126 3702
www.awwcookbooks.com.au

MEDIA GROUP

BAUER MEDIA BOOKS
Publisher - Sally Wright
Editorial & Food Director - Pamela Clark
Director of Sales, Marketing & Rights - Brian Cearnes
Creative Director - Hieu Chi Nguyen

Published and Distributed in the United Kingdom by Octopus Publishing Group
Endeavour House
189 Shaftesbury Avenue
London WC2H 8JY
United Kingdom
phone (+44)(0)207 632 5400; fax (+44)(0)207 632 5405
info@octopus-publishing.co.uk;
www.octopusbooks.co.uk

Printed by 1010 Printing International Limited, China.

International foreign language rights, Brian Cearnes, Bauer Media Books
bcearnes@bauer-media.com.au

A catalogue record for this book is available from the British Library.
ISBN: 978 174245 437 5 (paperback)